To
_____

From
_____

50 Daily Faith Confessions for My Daughter

DOTUN
OYEWOPO

50 Daily Faith Confessions for My Daughter

PUBLISHED IN AUSTRALIA BY
ACHIEVERS WORLD

50 Daily Faith Confessions for My Daughter
Copyright © 2020 by Dotun Oyewopo.
All rights reserved.

Requests for information should be addressed to:
dotunoyewopo@gmail.com

This book, or parts thereof, may not be reproduced, stored in a retrieval system, or transmitted in any form or by any means, electronic, mechanical, photocopying, recording or otherwise, without the written permission of the publisher.

ISBN 978-0-6487534-1-4 (paperback)
ISBN 978-0-6487534-2-1 (ebook)

Printed in Australia

Every attempt has been made to credit the sources of copyrighted material used in this book. If any such acknowledgment has been inadvertently omitted or miscredited, receipt of such information would be appreciated

Unless otherwise noted, all scriptures are from *The Holy Bible, New International Version*. Copyright © 1973, 1978, 1984, 2011 by Biblica, Inc.® Used by permission of Zondervan. All rights reserved worldwide. www.Zondervan.com.

Scripture quotations marked (KJV) are taken from the *King James Version of the Bible*.

Scripture quotations marked (NLT) are from the *Holy Bible, New Living Translation*. Copyright © 1996, 2004, 2007 by Tyndale House Foundation. Used by permission of Tyndale House Publishers Inc., Carol Stream, Illinois 60188. All rights reserved.

Scripture quotations marked (GW) are taken from GOD'S WORD® Copyright© 1995 by God's Word to the Nations. All rights reserved

Scripture quotations marked (MSG) are taken from *The Message*. Copyright © 1993, 1994, 1995, 1996, 2000, 2001, 2002 by Eugene H.Peterson.

Scripture quotations marked (GNT) are taken from the Holy Bible, Good News Translation. Copyright © 1992 by American Bible Society.

Scripture quotations marked (ISV) are taken from the Holy Bible, International Standard Version. Copyright © 1995–2014 by ISV Foundation. All rights reserved internationally. Used by permission of Davidson Press, LLC. S

Scripture quotations marked (ESV) are taken from the Holy Bible, English Standard Version, copyright © 2001 by Crossway Bibles, a division of Good News Publishers. Used by permission. All rights reserved.

Scripture quotations marked (CEV) are taken from Holy Bible: Contemporary English Version. Copyright © 1995 American Bible Society.

Scripture quotations marked (NAS) are taken from the New American Standard Bible , copyright © 1960, 1962, 1963, 1968, 1971, 1972, 1973, 1975, 1977, 1995 by the Lockman Foundation. Used by permission.

Scripture quotations marked (CSB) from the Holy Bible, The Christian Standard Bible. Copyright © 2017 by Holman Bible Publishers. Used by permission. All rights reserved.

Words and phrases in Scripture quotations that are in **bold** or *italics* are the emphasis of the author.

Dedication

This book is dedicated to all parents who are ready to ground the foundation of their daughters with faith confessions from their hearts.

This moment in your life is precious because God has destined that today, you will hold this book *50 Daily Faith Confessions for My Daughter*.

I believe, and I am convinced beyond any doubt that God wants us to ask boldly for His blessings on our daughters. God has promised to answer all of our requests if we ask Him in prayer.

"In that day you will no longer ask me anything. Very truly I tell you, my Father will give you whatever you ask in my name. Until now you have not asked for anything in my name. Ask and you will receive, and your joy will be complete"

(John 16:23-24, NIV).

Acknowledgment

I acknowledge the maker of heaven and the earth, the almighty God, the inspirational giver, the giver of visions and dreams, the giver of wisdom, knowledge, and understanding.

You gave me the book title, as well as wisdom and knowledge through the Holy Spirit. I couldn't have done it without You.

To my dearest husband, Oluwafemi Emmanuel Oyekunle Oyewopo, thank you for always supporting me. You are my hero. I love you, my husband.

To my sons King David Boluwatife Abisoye Oyewopo and Father Abraham Adekolade Ayodeji Oyewopo, I am grateful to you both. I thank you for your encouragement and daily support. I am so proud to be called your mother.

Forward

In this book, Pst Dotum has provided an impactful, convenient and focused way to pray specifically for our daughters. I love how each confession is paired with a relevant bible verse which is certainly going to stir up more prayer words from the readers. I think this is Powerful yet simple prayer guide and an essential tool in a prayer toolkit of anyone who is a mother to a girl.

Esther Matemba
An academic and a devoted mother of two boys.

REVIEW

Good daily confessions for daughters. It is also good to be used as daily prayers.

Pst Patricia Morgan

Original and Scripture-based prayer points speaking life into our children. This is a critical tool in this modern society where our children are exposed to harsh death pronouncements. I recommend these prayers to all parents. It is great encouragement to our young and older ones alike. This book may serve as a quick Scripture reference for personal edification. Congratulations once again my pastor and best friend.

Hope Kachila

An amazing book. I like the words of faith and the way you made it interactive. You are truly moving from glory to glory. God bless you.

Kudzai Magaya Chibanda

"The tongue has the power of life and death, and those who love it will eat its fruit"

— (Proverbs 8:21, NIV)

CONTENTS

Introduction 1
Power of Confession 1
Prayer for my Daughter 3
DAY 1 8
DAY 2 10
DAY 3 12
DAY 4 14
DAY 5 16
DAY 6 18
DAY 7 20
DAY 8 22
DAY 9 24
DAY 10 26
DAY 11 28
DAY 12 30
DAY 13 32
DAY 14 34
DAY 15 36
DAY 16 38
DAY 17 40
DAY 18 42

DAY 19	44
DAY 20	46
DAY 21	48
DAY 22	50
DAY 23	52
DAY 24	54
DAY 25	56
DAY 26	58
DAY 27	60
DAY 28	62
DAY 29	64
DAY 30	66
DAY 31	68
DAY 32	70
DAY 33	72
DAY 34	74
DAY 35	76
DAY 36	78
DAY 37	80
DAY 38	82
DAY 39	84
DAY 40	86
DAY 41	88

DAY 42	90
DAY 43	92
DAY 44	94
DAY 45	96
DAY 46	98
DAY 47	100
DAY 48	102
DAY 49	104
DAY 50	106
How to be Saved	108

INTRODUCTION

Power of Confession

Many believers do not understand confession—what it is and the power it has. Hence, we have not tapped into the full potential of our confessions. We have not seen or experienced the abundant promises of God in His Word.

Speaking the Word of God is completely different from confession. Therefore, it is important to understand the difference. Confession goes beyond simply speaking the Word. It is declaring what you are convinced of and hold to be true.

"The scripture says, 'I spoke because I believed.' In the same spirit of faith we also speak because we believe" (2 Corinthians 4:13, GNT).

With your heart, you believe and with your mouth, confession is made to salvation. You must watch what you say because your confession either brings life or death. Our mouths are very powerful, so are the words that come out of them. The words we speak are alive and active.

"Watch your words and hold your tongue; you'll save yourself a lot of grief" (Proverbs 21:23, MSG).

"Words kill, words give life; they're either poison or fruit— you choose" (Proverbs 18:21, MSG).

"You are snared by the word of your mouth; you are taken by the words of your mouth"

(Proverbs 6:2, MSG).

"Let no corrupt communication proceed out of your mouth, but that which is good to the use of edifying, that it may minister grace unto the hearers" (Ephesians 4:29, KJV).

Prayer for my Daughter

Daughters are beautiful blessings from the Lord. God's Word is the main source for training a godly girl to be a godly woman. Tell your daughter about Christ. Encourage her with the Bible so she can grow up to be a strong Christian woman.

I believe, and I am convinced beyond any doubt that God wants us to ask boldly for His blessing on our daughters.

We must ground our prayers in His Word. The Word of God is the solid foundation to stand on. When we do this, we can be assured we're praying according to His will.

Remind your daughter about the power of prayer and that God is always watching over her. Love your daughter and thank God for an amazing blessing.

God has promised to answer all of our requests if we ask Him in prayer. Our Lord made this known in His Word.

"In that day you will no longer ask me anything. Very truly I tell you, my Father will give you whatever you ask in my name. Until now you have

not asked for anything in my name. Ask and you will receive, and your joy will be complete" (John 16:23-24, NIV).

I pray that my daughter will always find her identity in Christ and remember that her purpose is to glorify Him.

"But you are a chosen generation, a royal priesthood, a holy nation, His own special people, that you may proclaim the praises of Him who called you out of darkness into His marvellous light" (1 Peter 2:9, NIV).

I pray that my daughter will love God and His Word and will turn to the Bible first for her answers. I pray that she will depend on the Word of God.

"With my lips I declare all the rules of your mouth. In the way of your testimonies I delight as much as in all riches. I will meditate on your precepts and fix my eyes on your ways. I will delight in your statutes; I will not forget your word" (Psalm 119:13-16, ESV).

I pray that my daughter will bring glory to God with all the gifts and talents she has been given by God. She will recognise them and put them to use for God.

"Each of you should use whatever gift you have received to serve others, as faithful stewards of God's grace in its various forms" (1 Peter 4:10, NIV).

I pray that my daughters will be like pillars carved to adorn a palace.

"May our sons flourish in their youth like well-nurtured plants. May our daughters be like graceful pillars, carved to beautify a palace" (Psalm 144:12, NLT).

I pray that my daughter will hunger and thirst for righteousness. God, You have promised to bless and satisfy those who hunger and thirst for righteousness.

"Blessed are those who hunger and thirst for righteousness, for they will be filled"

(Matthew 5:6, NIV).

I pray that You will pour out Your Spirit and Your blessings on my daughter.

"For I will pour water on the thirsty land, and streams on the dry ground I will pour out my Spirit on your offspring, and my blessing on your descendants"

(Isaiah 44:3, NIV).

God, I pray that You will bring my daughter to the saving knowledge and grace of our Lord Jesus Christ and help her to grow in the knowledge and love for Jesus.

"If you declare with your mouth, "Jesus is Lord," and believe in your heart that God raised him from the dead, you will be saved" (Romans 10:9, NIV).

God, I pray that You will guard my daughter's thought. I pray she will be protected from friends, behaviours, and addictions that would draw her heart away from You.

"Carefully guard your thoughts because they are the source of true life"

(Proverbs 4:23, CEV).

I pray that my daughter will seek You first in all her ways. She will make You her priority.

"But seek first his kingdom and his righteousness, and all these things will be given to you as well" (Matthew 6:33, NIV).

God, I pray that my daughter will draw nearer to You.

"Draw near to God and He will draw near to you. Cleanse *your* hands, *you* sinners; and purify *your* hearts, *you* double-minded" (James 4:8).

I pray that Your grace is sufficient for my daughter. Your power is made perfect in her weakness. I pray that Your power will rest on her.

"But he said to me, "My grace is sufficient for you, for my power is made perfect in weakness." Therefore I will boast all the more gladly about my weaknesses, so that Christ's power may rest on me" (2 Corinthians 12:9, NIV).

I pray that my daughter will live a righteous life. Place within her heart a longing for Your righteousness.

"If we confess our sins, He is faithful and righteous to forgive us our sins and to cleanse us from all unrighteousness" (1 John 1:9, NASB).

I pray that my daughter's words, actions, and life will be an outpouring of Your grace, giving life to those around her

"Let your conversation be always full of grace, seasoned with salt, so that you may know how to answer everyone" (Colossians 4:6, NIV).

I pray that my daughter will soar on wings like eagles; she will run and not grow weary, and she will walk and not faint.

"But those who hope in the Lord will renew their strength. They will soar on wings like eagles; they will run and not grow weary, they will walk and not be faint" (Isaiah 40:31, NIV).

I pray that my daughter will grow in wisdom, stature, and in favour with You and others.

"And Jesus grew in wisdom and stature, and in favor with God and man"

(Luke 2:52, NIV).

Daily Faith Confession

DAY 1

Today, I confess that my daughter is what the Word of God says she is.

"For we are God's MASTERPIECE.
He has created us anew in Christ Jesus, so we can do the good things he planned for us long ago"

(Ephesians 2:10, NLT).

Scriptural Reflection

(Ephesians 2:10, NLT)

Daily Faith Confession
DAY 2

Today, I confess that my daughter can do what the Word of God says she can do.

"I can do all things through Christ who strengthens me" (Philippians 4:13, NKJV).

Scriptural Reflection

(Philippians 4:13, NKJV)

Daily Faith Confession
DAY 3

Today, I confess that my daughter's life will not be wasted. She will live a meaningful life!

"The thief's purpose is to steal and kill and destroy. My purpose is to give them a rich and satisfying life"

(John 10:10, NLT).

Scriptural Reflection

(John 10:10, NLT)

Daily Faith Confession

DAY 4

Today, I confess that my daughter will succeed in everything she does. She will be fruitful in life.

"They are like trees that grow beside a stream, that bear fruit at the right time, and whose leaves do not dry up. They succeed in everything they do"

(Psalm 1:3, GNT).

Scriptural Reflection

(Psalm 1:3, GNT)

Daily Faith Confession
DAY 5

Today, I confess that my daughter is blessed. The favour of God will locate her.

"You bless righteous people, O LORD. Like a large shield, you surround them with your favour"

(Psalm 5:12, GW).

Scriptural Reflection

(Psalm 5:12, GW)

Daily Faith Confession
DAY 6

Today, I confess that the divine mercy of God will locate my daughter.

"The steadfast love of the Lord never ceases; his mercies never come to an end; they are new every morning; great is your faithfulness"

(Lamentations 3:22-23, ESV).

Scriptural Reflection

(Lamentations 3:22-23, ESV)

Daily Faith Confession

DAY 7

Today, I confess that doors of opportunity will open for my daughter.

"The LORD said to Cyrus, his chosen one: I have taken hold of your right hand to help you capture nations and remove kings from power. City gates will open for you; not one will stay closed"

(Isaiah 45:1, CEV).

Scriptural Reflection

(Isaiah 45:1, CEV)

Daily Faith Confession
DAY 8

Today, I confess that my daughter is like graceful pillars, carved to beautify a palace.

"May our sons flourish in their youth like well-nurtured plants. May our daughters be like graceful pillars, carved to beautify a palace"

(Psalm 144:12, NLT).

Scriptural Reflection

(Psalm 144:12, NLT).

Daily Faith Confession
DAY 9

Today, I confess that all my daughter's efforts shall be crowned with good success.

"The LORD will send rain at the proper time from his rich treasury in the heavens and will bless all the work you do. You will lend to many nations, but you will never need to borrow from them"

(Deuteronomy 28:12, NLT).

Scriptural Reflection

(Deuteronomy 28:12, NLT)

Daily Faith Confession
DAY 10

Today, I confess that my daughter shall not labour in vain.

"They won't build for others to inhabit; they won't plant for others to eat— for like the lifetime of a tree, so will the lifetime of my people be, and my chosen ones will long enjoy the work of their hands"

(Isaiah 65:22, ISV).

Scriptural Reflection

(Isaiah 65:22, ISV)

Daily Faith Confession
DAY 11

Today, I confess that my daughter's God-given talents will not be buried.

"For you will soon be bursting at the seams. Your descendants will occupy other nations and resettle the ruined cities"

(Isaiah 54:2-3, NLT).

Scriptural Reflection

(Isaiah 54:2-3, NLT)

Daily Faith Confession

DAY 12

Today, I confess that my daughter shall not eat the fruit of bitterness.

"Foreigners will be your servants. They will feed your flocks and plow your fields and tend your vineyards"

(Isaiah 61:5, NLT).

Scriptural Reflection

(2 Timothy 1:7, NKJV)

Daily Faith Confession
DAY 14

Today, I confess that my daughter has the Spirit of God. She is productive and intelligent.

"Then this Daniel distinguished himself above the governors and satraps, because an excellent spirit was in him; and the king gave thought to setting him over the whole realm"

(Daniel 6:3, NKJV).

Scriptural Reflection

(Daniel 6:3, NKJV) (Daniel 5:14, NKJV)

Daily Faith Confession

DAY 15

Today, I confess that my daughter will not do less than God's expectation for her life.

"My nourishment comes from doing the will of God, who sent me, and from finishing his work"

(John 4:34, NLT).

Scriptural Reflection

(John 4:34, NLT)

Daily Faith Confession
DAY 16

Today, I confess that my daughter is a champion! She was born to win!

"For if by the one man's offense death reigned through the one, much more those who receive abundance of grace and of the gift of righteousness will *reign in life* through the One, Jesus Christ"

(Romans 5:17, NKJV).

Scriptural Reflection

(Romans 5:17, NKJV)

Daily Faith Confession
DAY 17

Today, I confess that my daughter is efficient and effective.

"See, I will make you into a threshing sledge, new and sharp, with many teeth. You will thresh the mountains and crush them, and reduce the hills to chaff"

(Isaiah 41:15, NIV).

Scriptural Reflection

(Isaiah 41:15, NIV)

Daily Faith Confession

DAY 18

Today, I confess that
my daughter is not a failure.
She will not fall.

"No matter how often honest people fall, they always get up again"

(Proverbs 24:16, GNT).

Scriptural Reflection

(Proverbs 24:16, GNT)

Daily Faith Confession
DAY 19

Today, I confess that
my daughter is made for greatness.
She will be the head and not the tail.

"The LORD will make you the head and not the tail; you will only move upward and never downward"

(Deuteronomy 28:13, CSB).

Scriptural Reflection

(Deuteronomy 28:13, CSB)

Daily Faith Confession
DAY 20

Today, I confess that my daughter is divinely connected to helpers of destiny.

"Arise, shine, for your light has come, and the glory of the Lord rises upon you. Nations will come to your light, and kings to the brightness of your dawn"

(Isaiah 60:1, 3).

"Kings will be your foster fathers, and their queens your nursing mothers"

(Isaiah 49:23, NIV).

Scriptural Reflection

(Isaiah 60:1, 3) (Isaiah 49:23, NIV)

Daily Faith Confession

DAY 21

Today, I confess that my daughter shall not be disappointed. Her face will never be covered with shame.

"I sought the Lord, and he answered me; he delivered me from all my fears. Those who look to him are radiant; their faces are never covered with shame"

(Psalm 34:4-5, NIV).

Scriptural Reflection

(Psalm 34:4-5, NIV)

Daily Faith Confession
DAY 22

Today, I confess that my daughter shall eat the fruit of her labour. She will be prosperous in life.

"You will eat the fruit of your labour; blessings and prosperity will be yours"

(Psalm 128:2, NIV).

Scriptural Reflection

(Psalm 128:2, NIV)

Daily Faith Confession
DAY 23

Today, I confess that my daughter is secure. The goodness of God shall locate her.

"I waited patiently for the Lord's help; then he listened to me and heard my cry. He pulled me out of a dangerous pit, out of the deadly quicksand. He set me safely on a rock and made me secure"

(Psalm 40:1-3, GNT).

Scriptural Reflection

(Psalm 40:1-3, GNT)

Daily Faith Confession

DAY 24

Today, I confess that all my daughter's needs are divinely met.

"And my God shall supply all your needs according to His riches in glory by Christ Jesus"

(Philippians 4:19, NKJV).

Scriptural Reflection

(Philippians 4:19, NKJV)

Daily Faith Confession
DAY 25

Today, I confess that sickness is not my daughter's portion.

"So you shall serve the LORD your God, and He will bless your bread and your water. And I will take away sickness from among you"

(Exodus 23:25).

Scriptural Reflection

(Exodus 23:25)

Daily Faith Confession

DAY 26

Today, I confess that my daughter shall not be a victim of circumstances.

"He will cover you with his feathers, and under his wings you will find refuge;... You will not fear the terror of night, nor the arrow that flies by day, nor the pestilence that stalks in the darkness, nor the plague that destroys at midday"

(Psalm 91:4-6, NIV).

Scriptural Reflection

(Psalm 91:4-6, NIV)

Daily Faith Confession

DAY 27

Today, I confess that my daughter will not be humiliated or ridiculed. She will not be put to shame.

"Do not be afraid; you will not be put to shame. Do not fear disgrace; you will not be humiliated. You will forget the shame of your youth and remember no more the reproach of your widowhood"

(Isaiah 54:4, NIV).

Scriptural Reflection

(Isaiah 54:4, NIV)

Daily Faith Confession
DAY 28

Today, I confess that my daughter's joy shall know no bounds.

"You will show me the path of life; In Your presence is fullness of joy; At Your right hand are pleasures forevermore"

(Psalm 16:11, NKJV).

Scriptural Reflection

(Psalm 16:11, NKJV)

Daily Faith Confession
DAY 29

Today, I confess that my daughter is delivered from procrastination.

"For I can do everything through Christ, who gives me strength"

(Philippians 4:13, NLT).

Scriptural Reflection

(Philippians 4:13, NLT)

Daily Faith Confession

DAY 30

Today, I confess that my daughter is delivered from littleness. She will increase abundantly.

"For who has despised the day of small things?"

(Zechariah 4:10, NKJV).

"Though your beginning was small, yet your latter end would increase abundantly"

(Job 8:7, NKJV).

Scriptural Reflection

(Job 8:7, NKJV) (Zechariah 4:10, NKJV)

Daily Faith Confession
DAY 31

Today, I confess that my daughter is delivered from laziness.

"And we desire that each one of you show the same diligence to the full assurance of hope until the end, that you do not become sluggish, but imitate those who through faith and patience inherit the promises"

(Hebrews 6:11-12, NKJV).

Scriptural Reflection

(Ecclesiastes 9:10, NLV) (Hebrews 6:11-12, NKJV).

Daily Faith Confession

DAY 32

Today, I confess that my daughter's mind is renewed for greatness.

"Thou shalt increase my greatness, and comfort me on every side"

(Psalm 71:21, NKJV).

Scriptural Reflection

(Psalm 71:21, NKJV)

Daily Faith Confession

DAY 33

Today, I confess that my daughter has a focused mind to accomplish her vision in life.

"'For I know the plans I have for you,' declares the LORD, 'plans to prosper you and not to harm you, plans to give you hope and a future'"

(Jeremiah 29:11, NIV).

Scriptural Reflection

(Jeremiah 29:11, NIV)

Daily Faith Confession

DAY 34

Today, I confess that my daughter shall go from glory to glory.

"But we all, with open face beholding as in a glass the glory of the Lord, are changed into the same image from glory to glory, even as by the Spirit of the Lord"

(2 Corinthians 3:18, KJV).

Scriptural Reflection

(2 Corinthians 3:18, KJV)

Daily Faith Confession
DAY 35

Today, I confess that my daughter shall move forward in life.

"But the path of the just *is* as the shining light, that shineth more and more unto the perfect day"

(Proverbs 4:18).

Scriptural Reflection

(Proverbs 4:18)

Daily Faith Confession

DAY 36

Today, I confess that the Lord shall crown my daughter with favour.

"Surely, LORD, you bless the righteous; you surround them with your favor as with a shield"

(Psalm 5:12, NIV).

Scriptural Reflection

(Psalm 5:12, NIV)

Daily Faith Confession

DAY 37

Today, I confess that my daughter shall not be frustrated.

"These things I have spoken unto you, that in me ye might have peace. In the world ye shall have tribulation: but be of good cheer; I have overcome the world"

(John 16:33, KJV).

Scriptural Reflection

(John 16:33, KJV)

Daily Faith Confession

DAY 38

Today, I confess that my daughter will not be depressed.

"Why, my soul, are you downcast? Why so disturbed within me? Put your hope in God, for I will yet praise him, my Savior and my God"

(Psalm 42:11, NIV).

Scriptural Reflection

(Psalm 42:11, NIV)

Daily Faith Confession

DAY 39

Today, I confess that my daughter is delivered from anxiety.

"Therefore I tell you, do not worry about your life, what you will eat or drink; or about your body, what you will wear. Is not life more than food, and the body more than clothes? Look at the birds of the air; they do not sow or reap or store away in barns, and yet your heavenly Father feeds them. Are you not much more valuable than they? Can any one of you by worrying add a single hour to your life?"

(Matthew 6:25-27, NIV).

Scriptural Reflection

(Matthew 6:25-27, NIV)

Daily Faith Confession
DAY 40

Today, I confess that my daughter's future is colourful and bright.

"For I know the plans I have for you, declares the Lord, plans for welfare and not for evil, to give you a future and a hope"

(Jeremiah 29:11, ESV).

Scriptural Reflection

(Jeremiah 29:11, ESV)

Daily Faith Confession
DAY 41

Today, I confess that my daughter is endowed with divine wisdom.

"Blessed is the one who finds wisdom, and the one who gets understanding, for the gain from her is better than gain from silver and her profit better than gold. She is more precious than jewels, and nothing you desire can compare with her. Long life is in her right hand; in her left hand are riches and honor. Her ways are ways of pleasantness, and all her paths are peace"

(Proverbs 3:13-18, ESV).

Scriptural Reflection

(Proverbs 3:13-18, ESV).

Daily Faith Confession

DAY 42

Today, I confess that my daughter is endowed with divine understanding.

"For the Lord gives wisdom; from his mouth come knowledge and understanding"

(Proverbs 2:6, NIV).

Scriptural Reflection

(Proverbs 2:6, NIV)

Daily Faith Confession
DAY 43

Today, I confess that my daughter is endowed with divine knowledge.

"The Spirit of the LORD will rest on him— the Spirit of wisdom and of understanding, the Spirit of counsel and of might, the Spirit of the knowledge and fear of the LORD"

(Isaiah 11:2, NIV).

Scriptural Reflection

(Isaiah 11:2, NIV)

Daily Faith Confession
DAY 44

Today, I confess that my daughter is endowed with divine abilities.

"And God is able to make all grace abound to you, so that having all sufficiency in all things at all times, you may abound in every good work"

(2 Corinthians 9:8, ESV).

Scriptural Reflection

(2 Corinthians 9:8, ESV)

Daily Faith Confession

DAY 45

Today, I confess that my daughter is created to do good works.

"For we are God's handiwork, created in Christ Jesus to do good works, which God prepared in advance for us to do"

(Ephesians 2:10, NIV).

Scriptural Reflection

(Ephesians 2:10, NIV)

Daily Faith Confession

DAY 46

Today, I confess that my daughter's sun shall never set in the day.

"Thy sun shall no more go down, neither shall thy moon withdraw itself; for Jehovah will be thine everlasting light, and the days of thy mourning shall be ended"

(Isaiah 60:20, ASV).

Scriptural Reflection

(Isaiah 60:20, ASV)

Daily Faith Confession
DAY 47

Today, I confess that my daughter will shine and reign.

"Arise, shine; for your light has come, and the glory of the LORD has risen upon you"

(Isaiah 60:1, NAS).

Scriptural Reflection

(Isaiah 60:1, NAS)

Daily Faith Confession

DAY 48

Today, I confess that my daughter shall not mourn.

"And God shall wipe away all tears from their eyes; and there shall be no more death, neither sorrow, nor crying, neither shall there be any more pain: for the former things are passed away"

(Revelation 21:4, KJV).

Scriptural Reflection

(Revelation 21:4, KJV)

Daily Faith Confession
DAY 49

Today, I confess that my daughter is born to reign!

"God blessed them and said to them, "Be fruitful and increase in number; fill the earth and subdue it. Rule over the fish in the sea and the birds in the sky and over every living creature that moves on the ground"

(Genesis 1:28, NIV).

Scriptural Reflection

(Genesis 1:28, NIV)

Daily Faith Confession

DAY 50

Today, I confess that my daughter is coming out of shame to honour and praise!

"Do not be afraid, for you will not be put to shame; do not be humiliated, for you will not be disgraced. For you will forget the shame of your youth and remember no more the reproach of your widowhood"

(Isaiah 54:4).

Scriptural Reflection

(Isaiah 54:4)

How to be Saved

If you do not know God personally, here are four principles that will help guide you into a relationship with Him:

1. GOD LOVES YOU AND CREATED YOU TO KNOW HIM PERSONALLY.

The most well-known verse in the Bible says, *"God so loved the world, that he gave his only Son, that whoever believes in him should not perish but have eternal life"* **(John 3:16, ESV)**.

You see, this life is not the end of us. This life is preparation for eternity. We have the freedom to decide where we want to spend eternity: with God or apart from Him.

God thinks you're so valuable He wants to spend eternity with you! The Bible says, *"Now this is eternal life: that they may know you, the only true God, and Jesus Christ, whom you have sent"* **(John 17:3)**.

He planned the universe and orchestrated history, including the details of our lives, so that we could become His friends.

So, what prevents us from knowing God personally?

2. MAN IS SINFUL AND SEPARATED FROM GOD, SO WE CANNOT KNOW HIM PERSONALLY OR EXPERIENCE HIS LOVE BECAUSE OF OUR SINS.

The Bible says, *"All have sinned and fall short of the glory of God"* **(Romans 3:23)**.

Visualize God in heaven and man on the earth with a great gulf separating the two. Man is continually trying to reach God and establish a personal relationship with Him through his own efforts such as a good life, philosophy, or religion—but he inevitably fails.

The Bible says, "*The wages of sin is death* [separation from God]" **(Romans 6:23).** The third principle explains the only way to bridge this separation.

3. JESUS CHRIST IS GOD'S ONLY PROVISION FOR MAN'S SINS. THROUGH HIM ALONE CAN WE KNOW GOD PERSONALLY AND EXPERIENCE HIS LOVE.

JESUS DIED IN OUR PLACE.

"God demonstrates his own love for us in this: While we were still sinners, Christ died for us" **(Romans 5:8, NIV).**

HE ROSE FROM THE DEAD.

"Christ died for our sins, just as the Scriptures said. He was buried, and he was raised from the dead on the third day, just as the Scriptures said. He was seen by Peter and then by the Twelve. After that, he was seen by more than 500 of his followers at one time" **(1 Corinthians 15:3-6, NLT).**

HE IS THE ONLY WAY TO GOD.

"Jesus said to him, 'I am the way, and the truth, and the life; no one comes to the Father, but through Me'" **(John 14:6, NASB).**

Visualize now that God has bridged the gulf, which separates us from Him, by sending His Son Jesus Christ to die on the cross in our place to pay the penalty for our sins. Yet, it's not enough just to know these truths.

4. WE MUST INDIVIDUALLY RECEIVE JESUS CHRIST AS SAVIOR AND LORD; THEN WE CAN KNOW GOD PERSONALLY AND EXPERIENCE HIS LOVE.

WE MUST RECEIVE CHRIST.

"As many as received him, to them he gave the right to become children of God, even to those who believe in his name" **(John 1:12, NASB).**

WE RECEIVE CHRIST THROUGH FAITH.

"It is by grace you have been saved, through faith-and this not from yourselves, it is the gift of God-not by works, so that no one can boast" **(Ephesians 2:8–9, NIV).**

WHEN WE RECEIVE CHRIST, WE EXPERIENCE A NEW BIRTH.

The Bible tells of how a man named Nicodemus experienced new birth through Christ:

There was a man named Nicodemus, a Jewish religious leader who was a Pharisee. After dark one evening, he came to speak with Jesus. "Rabbi," he said, "we all know that God has sent you to teach us. Your miraculous signs are evidence that God is with you." Jesus replied, "I tell you the truth, unless you are born again, you cannot see the Kingdom of God." "What do you mean?" exclaimed Nicodemus. "How can an old man go back into his mother's womb and be born again?" Jesus replied, "I assure you, no one can enter the Kingdom of God without being born of water and the Spirit. Humans can reproduce only human life, but the Holy Spirit gives birth to spiritual life. So don't be surprised when I say, You must be born again. The wind blows wherever it wants. Just as you can hear the wind but can't tell where it comes from or where it is going, so you can't explain how people are born of the Spirit. **(John 3:1-8, NLT)**

WE RECEIVE CHRIST BY PERSONAL INVITATION

Jesus Christ says, *"Behold, I stand at the door and knock; if anyone hears my voice and opens the door, I will come in to him and dine with him, and he with me"* (Revelation 3:20, NASB)

Receiving Christ involves turning to God from self and trusting Christ to come into our lives to forgive us of our sins and to make us what He wants us to be. Just agreeing intellectually that Jesus Christ is the Son of God and that He died on the cross for our sins is not enough. Nor is it enough to have an emotional experience. We receive Jesus Christ by faith as an act of our free wills.

HOW YOU CAN RECEIVE CHRIST RIGHT NOW BY FAITH THROUGH PRAYER

Prayer is just talking with God. He knows your heart, so don't worry about getting your words just right. Here is a suggested prayer to guide you:

Lord Jesus, I want to know You personally. Thank You for dying on the cross for my sins.

I open the door of my life and receive You as my Saviour and Lord. Thank You for forgiving me of my sins and giving me eternal life. Take control of my life. Make me the kind of person You want me to be.

Does this prayer express the desire of Your heart? If it does, pray this prayer right now, and Christ will come into your life as promised.

Did you pray to receive Christ just now?

If so, congratulations! Luke 15:7 says that when one sinner accepts Jesus Christ as his or her Saviour, the angels rejoice. So there's a party going on in heaven right now over your decision! Remember this date as your "second birthday," the day you were born into a new life in Christ! You have God's Word that He answered your prayer.

The Bible promises eternal life to all who receive Christ: *"God has given us eternal life, and this life is in his Son. He who has the Son has the life; he who does not have the Son of God does not have the life. I write these things to you who believe in the name of the Son of God so that you may know that you have eternal life"* **(1 John 5:11–13, NIV).**

Thank God often that Christ is in your life and He will never leave you **(Hebrews 13:5)**.

You can know on the basis of His promise that Christ lives in you, and you have eternal life from the very moment you invited Him in.

Other book by Dotun Oyewopo

As glorious women, our self-worth should be based on the light of the knowledge God has shone into our hearts through His Word. The Word of God has clearly defined who we are and who we are not, what we are and what we are not.

Many women focus on their outward adornment; they are very concerned about how they look on the outside because that's what people can see. However, the Bible clearly states that your physical beauty is not the most important aspect of who you are. A lot of women place greater value on clothes, shoes, bags, cars, and jewellery than on the Holy Spirit inside them. Of course, it is easy to boast about the trappings and riches we have, but that is not what God sees as most significant when He looks at us.

The Glorious Woman is the secret to manifesting the beautiful woman in you. It helps you to know how you can influence your home, marriage, family, children, career, and ministry positively.

The Bible verses and prayer points will build, guide, and keep you focused.

Arise and shine daughter of God, for the glory of the Lord is risen upon you.

50 Daily Faith Confessions for My Son

Speak life into your son with these powerful daily confessions. What you say will boost his present and future. Do you want your son to reach his full potential? Do you wish him a life of good health, great relationships, and prosperity? Do you want him to live godly and reflect the character of God?

Boldly declare these confessions daily and invoke God's blessings on your son. Then watch the remarkable transformation. *Fifty Daily Faith Confessions for My Son* is an impactful prayer guide filled with original declarations and Scripture-based prayer points. It is grounded in the Word and helps you to focus on making specific, strategic proclamations.

In this ungodly world, our sons are struggling to live with purpose and purity and to find their identity. Condemnation, shame, guilt, lack of ambition, rebellion, and fear are haunting many lives. But you can help your son live to conquer. Make these declarations and help him overcome life's obstacles. He will become the man God wants him to be. Using these confessions is a great way to pray for your son no matter his age. Whether a toddler, teen, or adult, your words will be life-changing and potent. As you speak them, you will both experience the abundant promises of God in His Word.

You possess what you confess!

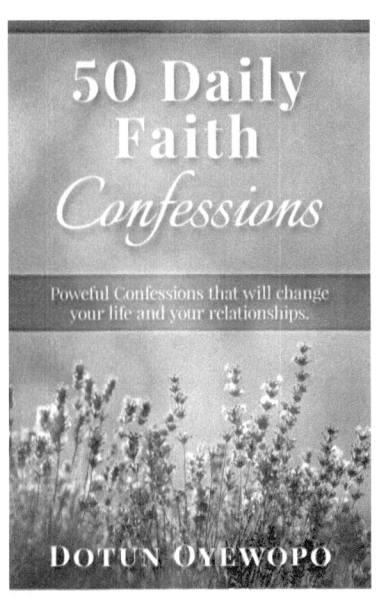

50 Daily Faith Confessions

Words are super powerful, alive, and active. They can inspire or tear down, work for or against you, condemn or set you free, heal or make you sick, get you in or out of trouble or give you life or death. Which will you choose?

Choose life! The *50 Daily Faith Confessions* will feed your mind, soul, and spirit with powerful truths based on Scripture. Each original declaration will help you set a solid foundation in your life. As you boldly speak, obstacles will move, generational curses broken, relationships restored, and your faith increased. You will experience protection, financial prosperity, daily provisions, and God's unmerited favor.

Practicing speaking positively about yourself creates a whole new world around you. It's a sure way to turn your life around as your mind and spirit are saturated and transformed by Scripture. Replace negative self-talk, self-condemnation, fear, and gloom with a narrative of life, faith, joy, and great possibilities. No matter what life throws your way, this powerful collection of faith declarations will empower, equip, and motivate you to overcome and live like a champion.

www.ingramcontent.com/pod-product-compliance
Lightning Source LLC
Chambersburg PA
CBHW020326010526
44107CB00054B/1990